I DARE YOU Not to YAWN

HÉLÈNE BOUDREAU
illustrated by SERGE BLOCH

WALKER BOOKS
AND SUBSIDIARIES
LONDON · BOSTON · SYDNEY · AUCKLAND

First published 2013 by Walker Books Ltd
87 Vauxhall Walk, London SE11 5HJ

This edition published 2014

2 4 6 8 10 9 7 5 3 1

Text © 2013 Hélène Boudreau
Illustrations © 2010 Serge Bloch

The right of Hélène Boudreau and Serge Bloch to be identified as author and illustrator respectively of this work
has been asserted by them in accordance with the Copyright, Designs and Patents Act 1988

This book has been typeset in Avenir Medium

Printed in China

British Library Cataloguing in Publication Data:
a catalogue record for this book is available from the British Library

ISBN 978-1-4063-5467-6

www.walker.co.uk

For Marcelle,
who was the first to dare me not to yawn
H. B.

Yawns are sneaky.
They can creep up on you when you least expect them.

There you are, minding your own business, building
the tallest block tower in the history of the universe
or dressing up the cat, when suddenly …

your arms stretch up, your eyes squish tight, your mouth opens wide, your tongue curls back and – *mmm … rrr … yawwrrrr* – a yawn pops out.

Next thing you know,
you're being sent upstairs
to put your pyjamas on!

Pyjamas lead to bedtime stories.

Bedtime stories lead to sleepy-time songs.

And sleepy-time songs lead to goodnight hugs and kisses.

Before you know it, you're tucked into bed,
snug as a bug, and wondering …

"How did I get here?"

So, if you're not ready to go to bed, follow these tips and DO NOT YAWN!

If someone else yawns, like your baby brother, or your big sister, or the dog – ahhh! – LOOK AWAY!

Yawns are like colds. They spread!

Stay away from huggable stuffed animals, soft cosy pyjamas and your favourite blankie, because – *mm … mm … mmm* – these can make you feel snuggly.

Avoid bedtime stories about sleepy baby animals, like tiger cubs arching their backs in one last stretch, their eyes squished tight and their tongues curled back – *rawr ... rawr ... rawr –*

or you might start to feel stretchy too.

Don't sing sleepy-time songs about twinkling stars or baaing sheep, especially the counting kind – one sheep, two sheep, *baa ... baa ... baaa...*

And WHATEVER YOU DO, don't think of a droopy-eyed baby orang-utan holding its long arms out for a hug from its mama,

its little mouth forming
a perfect o –
oh … oh … oh!

Uh-oh!

If you try all these things, but a yawn STILL creeps up
and grabs hold of you, QUICK, cover your mouth –
mmpprff! – to keep it from escaping.

Because if your arms stretch up –
mm ... mm ... mmm ...

your eyes squish tight –
rawr ... rawr ... rawrrr ...

your mouth opens wide –
baa ... baa ... baaa ...

your tongue curls back –
oh ... oh ... ohhh ...

and a yawn pops out –

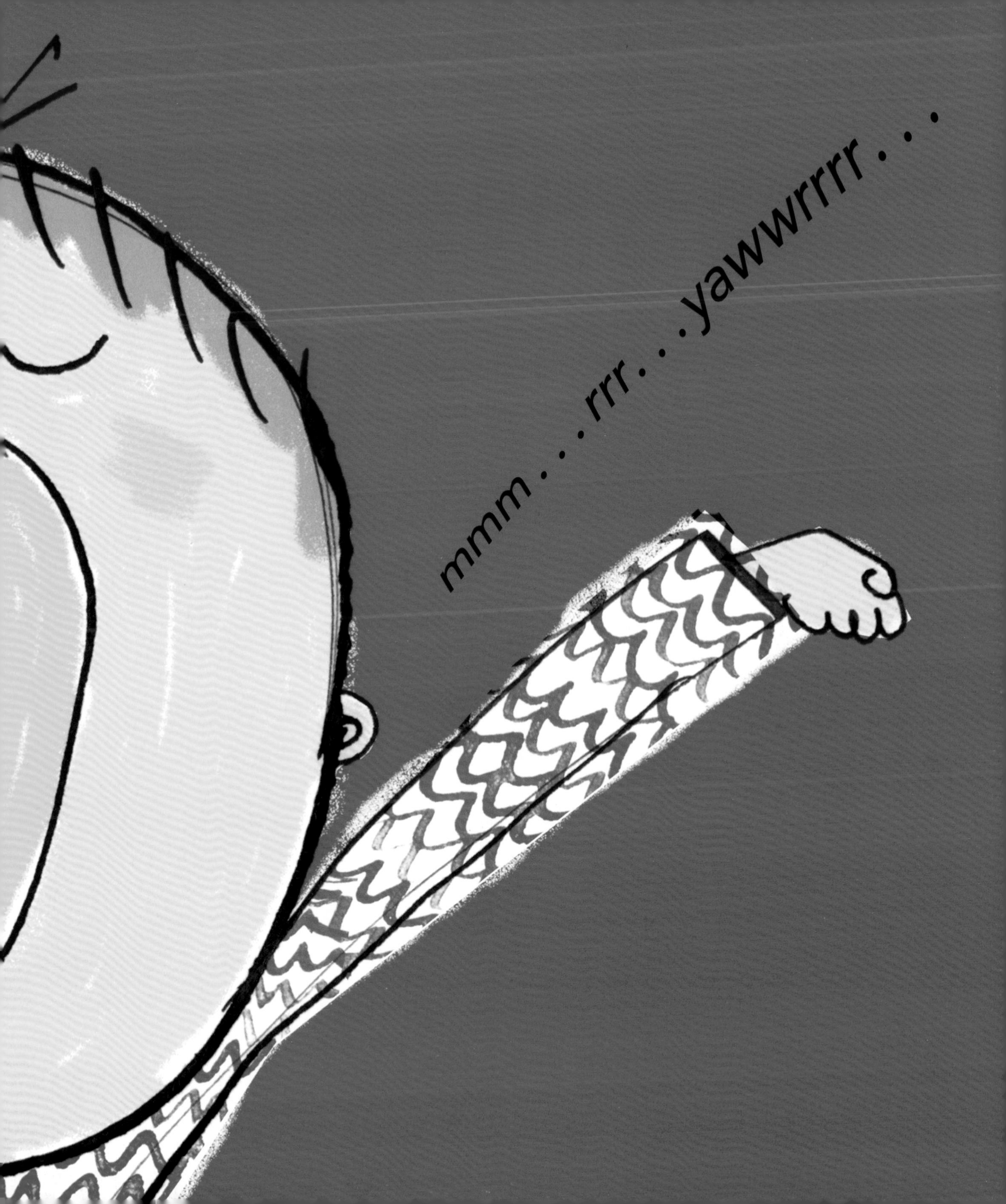
mmm. . .rrr. . .yawwrrrr. . .

then off to bed you'll go.

See? I told you.
Yawns are sneaky.